Insights into... Cancer

Henry W. Wright

Be in Health
4178 Crest Highway
Thomaston, Georgia 30286

www.beinhealth.com

EAN: 978-1-934680-10-0

Copyright Notice

Disclaimer

This ministry does not seek to be in conflict with any medical or psychiatric practices nor do we seek to be in conflict with any church and its religious doctrines, beliefs or practices. We are not a part of medicine or psychology, yet we work to make them more effective, rather than working against them. We believe many human problems are fundamentally spiritual with associated physiological and psychological manifestations. This information is intended for your general knowledge only. Information is presented only to give insight into disease, its problems and its possible solutions in the area of disease eradication and/or prevention. It is not a substitute for medical advice or treatment for specific medical conditions or disorders. You should seek prompt medical care for any specific health issues. Treatment modalities around your specific health issues are between you and your physician.

As pastors, ministers and individuals of this ministry, we are not responsible for a person's disease, nor are we responsible for his or her healing. All we can do is share what we see about a problem. We are not professionals; we are not healers. We are only ministers administering the Scriptures and what they say about this subject, along with what the medical and scientific communities have also observed in line with this insight. There is no guarantee that any person will be healed or any disease be prevented. The fruit of this teaching will come forth out of the relationship between the person and God based on these insights, given and applied. This ministry is patterned after the following: 2 Corinthians 5:18-20; 1 Corinthians 12; Ephesians 4; Mark 16:15-20.

Preface

This booklet was developed from a teaching to a live audience and has been kept in a conversational format. It is designed to reach a personal level with the reader rather than present a structured, theological presentation. Many times the reader will feel that Henry Wright is talking directly to him or her. The frequent use of the pronoun *you* is meant to penetrate the human heart for conviction, not for accusation.

TABLE OF CONTENTS

**BELOVED, I WISH ABOVE ALL THINGS
THAT THOU MAYEST PROSPER
AND BE IN HEALTH,
EVEN AS THY SOUL PROSPERETH.**

3 JOHN 1:2

The Curse of Cancer

Cancer is a feared word because mankind really does not understand what causes it. Mankind has some insight, and we will share part of that insight. Cancer does not happen just *because*... No disease happens *just because*...

All disease is a *curse*. Deuteronomy chapter 28 identifies it as a result of disobedience.

> **But it shall come to pass, if thou wilt not hearken unto the voice of the LORD thy God, to observe to do all his commandments and his statutes which I command thee this day; that all these curses shall come upon thee, and overtake thee:** Deuteronomy 28:15

Proverbs 26:2 says the curse causeless does not come.

> **As the bird by wandering, as the swallow by flying, so the curse causeless shall not come.** Proverbs 26:2

A few years ago I began to ask people who had disease: "Is your disease a blessing or a curse?"

Most people said, "A curse."

But when they went to their pastor, he said: "You're saved; you don't have a curse." They knew more about their state than their pastor did!

If anyone has a disease, it is a curse. The Bible says so, and most sheep say so. A person said to me, "Well, Pastor, I believe my disease is from God, and through the disease I have learned to come closer to Him."

I said, "It's a shame that it took a disease to get you closer to God."

We do not need to have disaster in our life to find God. We should find Him just like creation finds Him. Man is without excuse because creation demands that we acknowledge Him.

> **For the invisible things of him from the creation of the world are clearly seen, being understood by the things that are made, *even* his eternal power and Godhead; so that they are without excuse:** Romans 1:20

The trees have more sense than most humans.

CHRISTIAN HYPOCRISY

It is amazing how many Christians in America take the position their disease is from God. Many people say Cancer is from God. God is the author of life, not death. God does not tempt man with evil; neither can He be tempted with evil.

> **[13]Let no man say when he is tempted, I am tempted of God: for God cannot be tempted with evil, neither tempteth he any man:** James 1:13

An individual came to me saying; "Well, I just believe that my disease is from God and I'm suffering for Jesus."

I got serious. I said, "Are you going to a doctor?"

"Well, yes," he said.

I asked him, "Why?"

He said, "Well, I want to get well."

I said, "You hypocrite! How dare you interfere with God's will by trying to get well?"

This shows the shallowness of the theology.

Unknown Etiology

I am still learning about disease, and at BE IN HEALTH™ we have learned a lot. The American Medical Association (AMA) has stated that 30 percent of all Cancer has an unknown etiology (cause). They do not have any idea what causes it. *From observation over the years, whenever I have found the term "etiology unknown," I have found a spiritually-rooted disease.* This is almost without exception. The word "syndrome" attached to any biological breakdown is a spiritually-rooted disease.

Every syndrome is a spiritually-rooted disease

I constantly use my *Merck Manual* and a *Physician's Desk Reference.* The *Merck Manual* is about 2500 or 2600 pages of all that Satan has been doing to us in *his* blessing, which is the curse. It identifies all biological and psychological disease known to man. It is the *record* of the curse in mankind, what mankind sees about it, his modalities for management of it, his pharmacology protocol of it, his surgical procedures, etc.

As a pastor, I have to know not just what Theo (the Greek word for God) said, but as an under-shepherd, I also need to study what He created. Everything Satan has arrogantly made so visible through science, I am turning against him, including the benefits of billions of dollars of medical research that has been done to try to help man heal himself and his sin.

The church has just saved itself that amount of money in research because it is right there in the *Merck Manual*. Unfortunately, a lot of pastors do not know how to thoroughly read a biology book, much less this manual. Maybe if we are going to be under-shepherds of the Creator, it would be beneficial to know not just what He said, but also what He created.

CHROMOSOMES

In the *Merck Manual,* under the section "Cancer," we look at various issues such as chromosome abnormalities, which is an inherited genetic defect. That means the linking of the DNA and RNA is not normal in a specific chromosome.

On the wall of my office is a large chart of nearly 700 of the most well-known genetically inherited diseases and the chromosomal abnormality behind each one. There is a specific genetic defect, consistent with a specific disease, in a specific section of that chromosome, *every single time*.

For example, in bipolar disorder or manic depression, the x chromosome between the 24-27 A section is a genetically inherited bipolar recessive gene. It comes down the family tree through the mother. That genetic defect is consistent to that x chromosome, in that particular part of that chromosome, in *every single generation*.

Now, if Satan can change the genetic code defect through sin, guess Who can put it back in place the way it was from the foundation of the world? *The Living God through repentance can!*

We have verified changes in genetic code as a direct result of **BE IN HEALTH**™ and documented them with oncologists. In fact, I have a letter from an oncologist/geneticist who desperately wants to talk to me about how genetic code change can occur through prayer. Genetic impurity produces disease, and many of the Cancers we deal with involve genetic defect or chromosomal abnormality.

THE SIN BEHIND IT

A genetic defect can be caused by sin, spirits of death and spirits of infirmity, which are able to change the physiology of our bodies. We must never forget the models in Matthew, Mark, Luke, John and the book of Acts, which give us the ways Jesus ministered. Many times before Jesus healed someone of an incurable disease, He first cast out a spirit of Infirmity and *then* administered healing and miracles to the part of the body damaged by that spirit. We do not see that happening very often in prayer lines today because we just get out the bottle of oil. We need to read the *whole* Bible.

The Bible is a very simple gospel. We try to adhere as closely as we can to the models found in Matthew, Mark, Luke, John and the book of Acts. Today, we enjoy something they did not have—medical research—which helps us better understand our physiology.

Especially in Cancer, I would say to be prepared to remove a spirit of Death and a spirit of Infirmity. Sometimes behind Cancer lies a virus, so be prepared to remove it also.

Now we will address environmental factors that are behind chromosomal abnormalities.

ENVIRONMENTAL FACTORS

Cancer can also be caused by the introduction of chemicals to the body. These chemicals come from the outside and can include radiation, PCBs or any toxins of a concentrated nature. These could include carcinogens from a number of sources. So we now have the entrance of external chemicals that destroy the anti-oncogenes of the immune system. We refer to these as *environmental factors.*

Environmental factors are things we might be exposed to in our environment. Uncovered chemicals in the workplace are environmental factors. Those who have a fetish of smelling PCBs and popping transformer lids eventually will inhale enough PCBs to cause cellular genetic mutation.

Environmental factors could also include the ingesting of carcinogens, especially in those who smoke. Those who smoke are opening themselves to a spirit of death because they are bringing into their body a chemical that can help produce Cancer. Other environmental factors would include being exposed to the radiation from an exploding H-bomb, A-bomb or neutron bomb.

Classes of Cancer

Regarding the occurrence of Cancer, there are three classes of people. One class of people will never get Cancer. The second class is compromised or susceptible. The third class is totally vulnerable, and cell mitosis can begin at any time. Cell mitosis is Cancer. A cell splits and through a process called mitosis, goes from being one cell to becoming two. Those two cells split into 4, 8, 16, 32, etc., until a tumor is formed.

There are different classes of tumors. Some are considered malignant and others are considered benign. Both have their etiology, and both have their spirituality.

Now, in looking through some of the characteristics of Cancer and the entrance of external chemicals which cause toxicity, it is extremely important to know we can also experience toxicity internally. We can create toxins within our body. We are very chemical in our creation. We are comprised at the endocrine system level and the glandular level with little factories that manufacture various hormones, chemicals, neurotransmitters and so forth.

THE TOXINS WE CREATE

We can also create toxins. One spiritual dimension in which toxicity at the internal cellular level accelerates is

Bitterness. Hebrews tells us Bitterness can spring up and trouble us, defiling many. It is amazing that people who have Bitterness feel justified.

> **Looking diligently lest any man fail of the grace of God; lest any root of bitterness springing up trouble *you*, and thereby many be defiled.** Hebrews 12:15

Bitterness is the number one spiritual root to Toxicity

Bitterness is the number one spiritual root that produces toxicity internally at the cellular level. There is an old saying *"It eats at them like a Cancer."* We grind within ourselves; we begin to meditate on it. Then there is the *fear* issue because most of this is built around the failure of relationships. John says there is no fear in love.

> **There is no fear in love; but perfect love casteth out fear: because fear hath torment. He that feareth is not made perfect in love.** 1 John 4:18

Divine Health

Now we are going to talk about the aspect of fear (as in anxiety and stress) concerning Cancer as we move through this discussion. Again, this booklet is entitled *Insights into Cancer.* This is not only for our own life, but to help other people recover themselves also. God's perfect will is not to heal us. *God's perfect will is that we do not get sick.* Disease prevention is incredibly important. We will see that the same principles which move the hand of God to *heal* us are the same principles which, if we begin to apply them into our life daily, will *prevent* us from having many of the diseases that we might need prayer for later. So that is ***a more excellent way,*** which is the gospel.

> **But covet earnestly the best gifts: and yet shew I unto you a more excellent way.** 1 Corinthians 12:31

Deuteronomy 7 says that if we are obedient to God's commandments, observing, keeping and doing His word, He will put none of the diseases of Egypt upon us. In Deuteronomy 7 is a scripture that backs up the principle of divine health in the Old Testament.

> **Know therefore that the LORD thy God, he *is* God, the faithful God, which keepeth covenant and mercy with them that love him and keep his commandments to a thousand generations;** Deuteronomy 7:9

> **And the LORD will take away from thee all sickness, and will put none of the evil diseases of Egypt, which thou knowest, upon thee; but will lay them upon all *them* that hate thee.** Deuteronomy 7:15

Divine health is a scriptural principle which is also taught in the New Testament.

> **Beloved, I wish above all things that thou mayest prosper and be in health, even as thy soul prospereth.** 3 John 1:2

This scripture is especially for those who say, "Well, I believe healing passed away in Matthew, Mark, Luke, John and the book of Acts." Excuse me! This letter from the apostle John was written long after the book of Acts! He says, "I wish above all things that you prosper and be in good health." Is it God's will that we experience good health?

"Be in health, even as your soul prospers." This scripture also matches up with 1 Thessalonians 5:23, "May the God of peace sanctify you wholly..." God needs to make you *holy* so you can be *whole,* preserved blameless in spirit, soul, and body until the coming of the Lord Jesus.

> **And the very God of peace sanctify you wholly; and *I pray God* your whole spirit and soul and body be preserved blameless unto the coming of our Lord Jesus Christ.** 1 Thessalonians 5:23

This means it is a work of sanctification and cleansing and wholeness, here and now, in our generation, not someplace later when we get to heaven.

When people say someone they love died of Cancer and achieved a perfect healing in heaven, they do not realize something. When that person went into heaven, he did not receive a healing because he did not arrive in a bodily form. When we die, our bodies are in the dust, waiting for the resurrection. Our spirits, united with the consciousness of the soul, will be awaiting the resurrection in the 3rd heaven. That is what the Bible teaches.

So how could we achieve healing of a body that does not even exist? We have to wait for a glorified body in the day of the resurrection, which has not happened yet. Don't be bewitched by any futile or oral gospels that don't match Scripture.

Internal chemicals and toxicity can also cause Cancer. And there is also a contributing condition called Cell Wall Semi-Rigidity and Toxic Blood or Toxicity at the cellular level, which comes out of fear, anxiety and stress. Instead of the body cleansing itself as it was designed to do by God, cell wall rigidity causes the retention of toxins and waste by-products that are supposed to be expunged from our bodies and be released through elimination.

If those toxins are retained at the cellular level, it gives a foothold for cell *mutation* and allows the destruction of anti-oncogenes. Anti-oncogenes are immune sentries in every cell. Every cell has two; they are paired anti-oncogenes, which we will discuss later.

Health of the Immune System

The *Merck Manual* also supplies us with information on genetics and immunology. Immunology is the science of immune responses and involves the health of the immune system. A person with a compromised immune system coupled with a lowered white blood cell count is a candidate for Cancer.

The average person develops a rogue Cancer cell in the flow of their blood stream on the average of 200 times in a lifetime. Two hundred times! This is an American Medical Association (AMA) statistic. In a healthy immune system, Cancer just does not happen.

I want to explain some of the mechanisms that Satan uses to get access to our lives. He knows us very well! According to AMA statistics, if we have a healthy immune system, and one of those rogue Cancer cells attaches itself to tissue with a blood supply to feed it allowing growth, the statistical probability for Cancer to happen is one in 1,000,000.

On the other hand, a compromised immune system will not have enough T cells to defeat the rogue Cancer cell. Instead of having a T cell count in the range of at least 1,500 to 2,000, the count in a compromised immune system may be 700 or less. In that case, the chances of that rogue Cancer cell docking, finding a home and creating a tumor is very, very, very probable.

Likewise, the release of cortisol can adversely affect the body's ability to recognize rogue Cancer cells. Cortisol is released in conjunction with fear, anxiety and stress around any issue. If a person stays at a high level of fear, the cortisol can destroy an immune system, shutting down and devaluing interleukin-2, which identifies other cells as either friend or foe.

When that happens, the white corpuscles do not recognize the antigen flag on the Cancer cell. Instead they wave at it and say, "Hello Cancer, welcome to the body. Thank you for coming. Have a nice day!"

The white corpuscles of a compromised immune system will not recognize the Cancer cell as an enemy. Satan knows that if he can get us down to a certain level *spiritually,* he can cause us to become vulnerable *physically*. It's time to be educated so people will not perish for lack of knowledge!

> **My people are destroyed for lack of knowledge: because thou hast rejected knowledge, I will also reject thee, that thou shalt be no priest to me: seeing thou hast forgotten the law of thy God, I will also forget thy children.** Hosea 4:6

Metastasizing Cancer cells do not stand a chance with a healthy immune system. I was reading a *Discover* Magazine article by Dr. Stephen Rosenberg, the head of the National Cancer Institute for the last 30 years. The title of the article is, "I Have Seen Cancers Disappear." This Cancer research involves a case history of a man who was not a Christian yet was healed of Cancer.

Righteousness of the Unsaved

Have you ever wondered why unsaved people sometimes have better health than Christians? Just because someone is a Christian does not mean that person is righteous. There are some very evil Christians, and there are some very righteous unsaved people who have lived according to their conscience. They will receive their reward here, in their generation, without eternal salvation. Scripture says the rain falls on the just and the unjust.

> **That ye may be the children of your Father which is in heaven: for he maketh his sun to rise on the evil and on the good, and sendeth rain on the just and on the unjust.** Matthew 5:45

God honors His Word. We may not like that, but He honors His Word and He also honors the hearts of men. To every man has been given a measure of faith—the saved as well as the unsaved. If not, how could anyone ever become saved?

> **For I say, through the grace given unto me, to every man that is among you, not to think *of himself* more highly than he ought to think; but to think soberly, according as God hath dealt to every man the measure of faith.** Romans 12:3

We do not like to believe that the unsaved can do more righteous deeds than we, the saved, can do. It bothers us, doesn't it? It ought to!

Dr. Rosenberg came across an individual in 1968 whose immune system might hold the key to Cancer. While Dr. Rosenberg was working at the Veteran's Hospital in West Roxbury, Massachusetts, a grizzled 63-year-old man came in complaining of abdominal pain. Rosenberg found that he needed his gallbladder removed, but the man's medical history posed a mind-boggling question. Why was he still alive?

Twelve years earlier, the man had come in complaining of pain that turned out to be a huge malignant tumor in his stomach. The Cancer had also hardened his lymph nodes and infiltrated his liver. At that time, the surgeons opened him up, saw the tumors were inoperable, and sent him home to die. Yet here he was, 12 years later, complaining about his gallbladder.

When Rosenberg operated, he looked around everywhere in the man's abdominal cavity for signs of the tumor. There was nothing but soft, pink, healthy tissue. This case led him into a study of Cancer immunology. Something in that man's life happened, and his immune system strengthened. Maybe he faced death and lost the fear of it. We need to be very careful about fear of Cancer!

The Fear of Cancer

I want to read a couple of articles. The first one is from an editorial in *The New England Journal of Medicine,* December 18, 1975.

> Unfortunately when it comes to cancer, American society is far from rational. We are possessed with fear. But it is not only a matter of simple fear, Cancer-phobia has expanded into a demonism in which the evil spirit is ever present but furtively reviewed and spoken of obliquely. American cancer-phobia, in brief, is a disease as serious to society as cancer is to the individual and morally more devastating.

Remember the story of Job in Job 3?

> **[24]For my sighing cometh before I eat, and my roarings are poured out like the waters.**
> **[25]For the thing which I greatly feared is come upon me, and that which I was afraid of is come unto me.**
> **[26]I was not in safety, neither had I rest, neither was I quiet; yet trouble came.** Job 3:24-26

What was Job's fear? His fear was that his God would be ticked off at his children because they were party animals. Now Job had no Bible and no Word of God. In fact, theologians say Job was probably a contemporary of Abraham who served God out of his conscience. He was within Abraham's time, perhaps 435 years after the flood. So in that mixing of the generations after the flood, in the seed of Noah, Ham, Shem and Japheth, Job probably would have carried the knowledge of judgment. Who knows? It is not clear. There are no scriptures quoted because there were no scriptures in existence.

So Job served God out of a pure heart, a good conscience. Was Job sinless? No, Job was not sinless; the Bible is very clear on this. There is none righteous except Jesus Christ, the man. There was no other sinless man except for Adam and Eve, until they sinned. Everyone else is a sinner and has sin.

> **As it is written, There is none righteous, no, not one:** Romans 3:10

What Job feared actually came upon him and it creates the foundation for the law. Moses, 435 years later, became the giver of the law and God began to show us what evil and good looked like. Paul said through the law came the knowledge of sin.

> **Therefore by the deeds of the law there shall no flesh be justified in his sight: for by the law *is* the knowledge of sin.** Romans 3:20

Fear and faith are equal in this dimension: both project into the future, and both demand to be fulfilled. Fear can destroy our immune system. *Fear can set into motion the very thing that we are afraid of.*

The Bible has the record of it in Job 3. Some may say, "But I don't believe the Old Testament." I tell them what the New Testament says: the Old Testament scriptures are for our instruction in righteousness.

> **All scripture *is* given by inspiration of God, and *is* profitable for doctrine, for reproof, for correction, for instruction in righteousness:** 2 Timothy 3:16

Paul taught us through the law came the knowledge of sin. He taught us that those able to handle strong meat have exercised their senses through practical application and are able to discern both good and evil.

> **13For every one that useth milk *is* unskilful in the word of righteousness: for he is a babe.**
> **14But strong meat belongeth to them that are of full age, *even* those who by reason of use have their senses exercised to discern both good and evil.** Hebrews 5:13-14

I am against disease management. I stand 100 percent as a human being, as a believer and servant of the living God for the healing, prevention and eradication of all disease on this planet. To that end, I am dedicated!

Let me read something else. This is from Charles R. Shaw, Professor of Biology and Chief of the Medical Genetic Section at the University of Texas, M.D. Anderson Hospital and Tumor Institute in Houston.

> The goal is prevention of cancer. Cancer specialists have long recognized that this is the best approach to the control of cancer. One often hears the question, "Do you think we'll come up with a cure for cancer soon?" The more relevant question is, "Do you think we'll come up with a prevention of cancer soon?"

Understanding what causes Cancer is the only route to prevention.

My Mother's Testimony

When I was in my mother's womb, she was dying of Fibrosarcoma Cancer. Her mother had died of Cancer shortly after giving birth to her. My mother was raised by her natural father's brother, her uncle, as if she was a daughter, and they had other children.

My mother's Cancer was fast growing and fatal. It had wrapped around her jugular vein, up and down her neck into the base of her brain. When I was two months old, she was totally paralyzed and could not care for me, so they hired a nanny.

My parents were ministers; they were pioneer pastors in Hatfield's Point, New Brunswick, Canada. My mother was dying and there was no hope. There was nothing they could do. There was no surgery. It was impossible. It was incurable. It was just a matter of waiting it out until she died.

All manner of people had prayed for her, but she was not well. Even in her condition, she insisted on being carried on a stretcher to church services so she could lie in the front and be part of the services. That is dedication.

Several years ago, Donna and I had the pleasure of having dinner with Lee and Helen Boyd of Hatfield's Point, New Brunswick, Canada. I grew up with their son, Carl, and their daughters. I am using their names in this teaching because they were eyewitnesses to my mother's healing. They were in that service when the invisible, living God reached down out of nowhere and plucked masses of Cancer out of my mother as though it never existed. She had no special nutrition, no surgery, and no chemo. No one was even praying for her at that time.

These two eyewitnesses told me it was one of those services they could not get off the ground. Some of us may have been in that kind of service where nothing was happening. You see, as a child, I grew up with the testimony of God's healing power, but I had not heard this part of the testimony before. I had heard this testimony of my mother's healing all of my life, but I was not told this part of the story.

In that church service was a man who had harbored Bitterness against another man across town for twenty years. He stood up at the front of the church in that dead, dead service, and said, "This service is cursed because of me. I have had Bitterness in my heart for twenty years toward a man across town and God's not going to bless me, or you or anybody in this church until I get it right. I will see you later. I am out of here."

People began to repent, one to another. Knowing a little bit about my father today, I would say, even in that first year of marriage, my mother probably had developed a massive case of Bitterness because I had a very difficult father. I am suggesting that because the whole place erupted in repentance and forgiveness.

Growing up, I heard my mother had made a Hannah-type covenant. If God would heal her of the Cancer, she would raise me in the nurture and admonition of the Lord. In that meeting, paralyzed and on a stretcher, no one prayed for her. It was just her, God and silence, with everyone else doing what they were doing, when something happened. She connected with the invisible God without even trying.

Something happened. Maybe she forgave my father. Who knows what she was thinking? She came off that stretcher, unaided, from paralyzed to non-paralyzed, and she ran around the church shouting at the top of her lungs, "I'm healed! I'm healed! I'm healed!"

I was told the people's mouths were hanging open as they watched her run around and around and around. She would go up to them, take their hands, and thrust them up to heaven saying, "Praise Him!" "Praise Him!" "Praise Him!" She lived another 34 years, disease free. She was the only light I had as a child in my home while I was growing up. The rest was straight out of hell even though I was a preacher's kid.

What happened? The Cancer disappeared! Now that is a testimony!

Those who saw Sid Roth interview me on *It's Supernatural* also saw "before" and "after" pictures of the lady with Cancer on her face. When she repented of Bitterness, the tumor fell right off, and in less than a month, the skin underneath was back to normal.

A Lady with Tumors in Both Breasts

When I was teaching in Wycliffe, North Carolina, a lady was in the audience who had lumps in both of her breasts. She heard my teaching on Cancer in that conference.

One of the things we have seen in Cancer is the separation and breakdown of relationship between the female who has Breast Cancer—or lumps or tumors—and another female. This could be her mother, sisters, mother-in-law, or another close female. In this case she had simmering Bitterness against her mother *and* her mother-in-law.

I was teaching there for three days, but she did not come to me. She never said a word to me. I never even talked to her or prayed with her, but she went home from that conference thoroughly convicted.

She went into her prayer closet and began to repent to God for Bitterness against her mother. Then in her mind, these words formed, *"You need to not just repent, you need to go to your mother and make it right."* So she made an appointment with her mother and admitted this long-term Bitterness, irritation and resentment. She made her peace with her mother.

When she was rechecked by her doctor, all lumps were gone—but in her left breast only. She went back into her prayer closet and said, "God, why only one breast?" Again in her mind these words formed, *"You've only done half the work. What about your mother-in-law?"* Whoopsee daisy!

Then she made an appointment with her mother-in-law and went to her. She took responsibility, repented and made her peace with her mother-in-law. When she was rechecked by her doctor, all lumps had disappeared in the right breast! This was over 10 years ago, and she is well today. She is an active servant for the Lord.

No one prayed for her. No one prayed for my mother. Sometimes it is not necessarily prayer we need. Getting right with God, our brother and ourselves is what we need.

Case histories are providing documentation for this insight. We have seen that cysts or tumors in the left breast tissue seem to follow Bitterness and conflict between that female and another female who is a blood relative, such as mother, sister, aunt or grandmother. Tumors or cysts in the right breast seem to be the result of unresolved Bitterness and conflict between that female and a non-blood relative: someone such as a mother-in-law or a female in the workplace or church.

A Breach of Relationship

God intended for this planet to be inhabited in righteousness! He intended from the foundation of the world that we love our God with all of our heart and all of our soul and all of our might and we shall love our neighbor as ourselves. Upon this, all of the law and the prophets hang.

The basic foundation of the gospel is *relationship.*

> **37Jesus said unto him, Thou shalt love the Lord thy God with all thy heart, and with all thy soul, and with all thy mind.**
> **38This is the first and great commandment.**
> **39And the second *is* like unto it, Thou shalt love thy neighbour as thyself.**

> **[40]On these two commandments hang all the law and the prophets.** Matthew 22:37-40

I consider at least 30 percent of all Cancer to be the result of a fragmenting of love in relationships. The Bible says when we hate our brother, even when we speak against our brother with our tongue, we are a murderer. When we hate our brother without a cause, we are a murderer. Under the law, the penalty for murder was death. Now we can understand why a spirit of death is on the loose.

> **Whosoever hateth his brother is a murderer: and ye know that no murderer hath eternal life abiding in him.** 1 John 3:15

> **But I say unto you, That whosoever is angry with his brother without a cause shall be in danger of the judgment: and whosoever shall say to his brother, Raca, shall be in danger of the council: but whosoever shall say, Thou fool, shall be in danger of hell fire.**
> Matthew 5:22

It is very, very important we understand this. I have decided as an act of my will to forgive all men of all their sins forever. I refuse to take someone else's sin into my body or spirit. It is dangerous to my health! I have decided to be a man of peace. It may be surprising at times, the way I act, because my family calls me Mister Crash, Boom, Thud. People will always know when I am around, even though I am a quiet guy!

Psalm 120 says, I am for peace but my words, they are for war. Our battle is not against flesh and blood but against principalities, powers and spiritual wickedness in high places.

I am for peace: but when I speak, they are for war.
Psalm 120:7

For we wrestle not against flesh and blood, but against principalities, against powers, against the rulers of the darkness of this world, against spiritual wickedness in high *places*. Ephesians 6:12

According to 1 John 4, when we become separated from each other, we become separated from God, too. We cannot have fellowship with God and not have fellowship with our brother. We cannot say we love God and hate our brother. The truth is not within us.

If a man say, I love God, and hateth his brother, he is a liar: for he that loveth not his brother whom he hath seen, how can he love God whom he hath not seen? 1 John 4:20

He that saith, I know him, and keepeth not his commandments, is a liar, and the truth is not in him.
1 John 2:4

God is not going to have a relationship with us if we do not have a relationship with our brother. God is no respecter of persons, and He is going to shut down and sit down until we get this message straight.

Then Peter opened *his* mouth, and said, Of a truth I perceive that God is no respecter of persons: Acts 10:34

Some defend themselves, saying, "Well, you just don't know what that person did to me."

My answer is, "I know what *He did* for us."

I want the Word of God to pierce us deeply. There is a prophetic statement in Zechariah 13 that refers to a time not yet here. We can find this time also referenced in Ezekiel 40-48 when the King is on His throne in Jerusalem. All the nations are coming up to acknowledge the King of kings and Lord of lords.

> **And it shall come to pass, *that* every one that is left of all the nations which came against Jerusalem shall even go up from year to year to worship the King, the LORD of hosts, and to keep the feast of tabernacles.**
> Zechariah 14:16

These are the natural people we will rule over as kings and priests in the millennium. They have come out of great tribulation from many nations, including Egypt and the islands of the sea.

> **And it shall come to pass in that day, *that* the Lord shall set his hand again the second time to recover the remnant of his people, which shall be left, from Assyria, and from Egypt, and from Pathros, and from Cush, and from Elam, and from Shinar, and from Hamath, and from the islands of the sea.** Isaiah 11:11

Zechariah 13 says Egypt refuses to acknowledge the king until He broke them with famine. They were so rebellious!

> **And if the family of Egypt go not up, and come not, that *have* no *rain*; there shall be the plague, wherewith the LORD will smite the heathen that come not up to keep the feast of tabernacles.** Zechariah 14:18

In the millennium, according to this prophecy, natural man will come up to see the King and the prophet Zechariah. Their questions and Jesus' response is recorded by the Spirit of God through the prophet Zechariah, long in advance. It is years down the road from today.

Here is the question and the answer. They say, "Sir, where did you get these wounds that we see?" He answers, "These are the wounds I received in the house of my friends." So what is our problem? Have we been wounded in the house of our friends? The enemies of a man are in his own house.

> **And *one* shall say unto him, What *are* these wounds in thine hands? Then he shall answer, *Those* with which I was wounded *in* the house of my friends.**
> Zechariah 13:6

> **And a man's foes shall be they of his own household.** Matthew 10:36

A prophet is without honor in his own country.

> **And they were offended in him. But Jesus said unto them, A prophet is not without honour, save in his own country, and in his own house.** Matthew 13:57

So what is the deal? Have we made man our idol? Whether he approves of us, or likes us, or does not like us determines how we think. That is idolatry. We know the penalty for idolatry under the law was death.

Galatians 6 tells us we will reap what we sow, whether life unto life or death unto death.

> **8For he that soweth to his flesh shall of the flesh reap corruption; but he that soweth to the Spirit shall of the Spirit reap life everlasting.**
> **9And let us not be weary in well doing: for in due season we shall reap, if we faint not.** Galatians 6:8-9

Do you want love? Give it. Do you want a friend? Be a friend. Blessed are the pure in heart for they shall see God. Blessed are the merciful for they shall obtain mercy.

> **3Blessed *are* the poor in spirit: for theirs is the kingdom of heaven.**
> **4Blessed *are* they that mourn: for they shall be comforted.**
> **5Blessed *are* the meek: for they shall inherit the earth.**
> **6Blessed *are* they which do hunger and thirst after righteousness: for they shall be filled.**
> **7Blessed *are* the merciful: for they shall obtain mercy.**
> **8Blessed *are* the pure in heart: for they shall see God.**
> **9Blessed *are* the peacemakers: for they shall be called the children of God.** Matthew 5:3-9

I want to read some of the characteristics of the beatitudes listed in Matthew 5. These are the "be-attitudes" and the antidote for disease, with Cancer at the top of the list. Blessed are the meek for they shall inherit the earth. Blessed are the merciful for they shall obtain mercy. If you want mercy, give it. Blessed are the pure in heart for they shall what? See God.

Blessed are the peacemakers for they shall be called the children of God. I want to be a peacemaker. How about you?

You are either part of the solution or part of the pollution

I have decided to be part of the solution for the rest of eternity, not the pollution!

If you want forgiveness, give it. Do you want a smile? Give one. I heard something cute coming down the road, that a frown is just a smile turned upside down. I thought about it and said, "That's true." We need to get our smiles right-side up.

The Bible says love does not pay attention when wrong is done to it. It is long suffering. It is kind. It does not have envy and jealousy. It does not puff itself up or vaunt itself. It does not behave itself unseemly. It does not seek its own place. It is not easily provoked. Love thinks no evil, rejoices not in iniquity, but rejoices in truth, bears all things, believes all things, hopes in all things, endures all things.

> **4Charity suffereth long, *and* is kind; charity envieth not; charity vaunteth not itself, is not puffed up,**
> **5Doth not behave itself unseemly, seeketh not her own, is not easily provoked, thinketh no evil;**
> **6Rejoiceth not in iniquity, but rejoiceth in the truth;**
> **7Beareth all things, believeth all things, hopeth all things, endureth all things.** 1 Corinthians 13:4-7

Is that too hard? Well, if we look at our families and our churches, it is very hard.

Deadly Emotions

I want to read an article here from Dr. Don Colbert about Cancer prevention. You may have heard of him from TBN and places like that. At times, he recommends our ministry to his patients. He has our material and has given it to several well-known ministries in America.

I want to read what Dr. Colbert has to say about Cancer prevention. This is from CBN, dated July 2, 2001:

> One out of every three Americans will develop cancer at some time in their lifetime. One out of six will

actually die. Nothing strikes fear more in a patient than the diagnosis of cancer. Let me say that, yes, nutrition, vitamins and lifestyle changes are critically important in preventing cancer and in helping us through cancer, but before we discuss nutrition, let's look at *Deadly Emotions*.

Again, quoting Dr. Colbert:

> Many times cancer is associated with bitterness, resentment, unforgiveness and hatred and especially, guilt and shame. These emotions will actually cause a body to produce toxic material. They will increase cortisol levels which in turn will weaken the immune system and allow cancer to begin to form in the body.

As we can see, we need to forgive anyone who has wronged us, and we need to ask for forgiveness. We need to have a merry heart; we cannot be bitter. We cannot be angry; we have to start laughing! We have to start enjoying life. Most Cancer patients do not laugh and have difficulty with humor. The Bible says a merry heart doeth good like a medicine, but a broken spirit drieth up the bones. *That is the immune system.*

> **A merry heart doeth good *like* a medicine: but a broken spirit drieth the bones.** Proverbs 17:22

Laughter is the best medicine for overcoming Cancer because it actually helps to stimulate the immune system and the natural killer cells. Get rid of fear, put off the spirit of Heaviness, put on the garment of praise. The Bible says that the spirit of a man shall sustain him in his infirmity.

> **To appoint unto them that mourn in Zion, to give unto them beauty for ashes, the oil of joy for mourning, the garment of praise for the spirit of heaviness; that they might be called trees of**

righteousness, the planting of the LORD, that he might be glorified. Isaiah 61:3

The spirit of a man will sustain his infirmity; but a wounded spirit who can bear? Proverbs 18:14

"Spirit man, wake up! Get up! Take your place in the land of the living." That's what I tell people who have Cancer. Get up! Stand up, spirit man! Take your place in the land of the living. According to your faith be it unto you.

Then touched he their eyes, saying, According to your faith be it unto you. Matthew 9:29

So there is something that has to happen for Cancer to be defeated. You must have the will to live! You must stop being hopeless, waiting for the fatalistic end of some conclusion. Get *out* of self-pity. It' is the super glue of hell that binds us to the past. Encourage yourself in the Lord. Get *up*! Stand up!

Sometimes I have to get myself up to get before an audience. I have those days when the enemy comes for breakfast, and he does not have Cheerios with him. He has mully grubs with sour milk. Usually, I am up and ready to go. I do not get up and say, "Whoa, my God, another day." But in those moments, when I *have* those moments, I get myself up spiritually and say, "GET UP, HENRY!" "GET UP, HENRY!" "GET UP, YOU SON OF GOD!" "GET UP, GET UP! GET UP AND GET GOING!"

That is encouraging yourself in the Lord. I am a dead man already, and dead men are just happy to be alive. I will fulfill the call of God in my life and in my generation that God saw from the foundation of the world. When I have finished that call deep inside me, I will lay my own spirit down, thank you very much.

We need that dedication. Are we just treading water or waiting to get to that mystical place called heaven where we can have our rest? If I were God, I would send us back down here as fast as we got there. I'd say, "What are you doing here? I do not need you here. You are of no earthly good in heaven."

When Jesus taught the disciples to pray, He said, "Thy will be done on earth as it is in heaven." Why do we want to go up there when what is in heaven is supposed to be here?

> **Thy kingdom come. Thy will be done in earth, as *it is* in heaven.** Matthew 6:10

Nutrition certainly is important, but nutrition alone is not the answer to healing or disease prevention. I can put nutrition in the body to help the immune system, but destroy it in the process because of fear. The kingdom of God is not what you eat! It is not meat nor drink but righteousness, peace and joy in the Holy Ghost.

> **For the kingdom of God is not meat and drink; but righteousness, and peace, and joy in the Holy Ghost.**
> Romans 14:17

Stress Hormones

The following quote is from *Discovery Health* dated August 21, 2000.

> The stress hormone is linked to earlier death in women with breast cancer. Abnormal fluctuations in the stress hormone cortisol are linked to a decreased survival time with advanced breast cancer.

It is very, very important that we understand about fear, anxiety and stress, especially around the body's cortisol response. With Cancer comes the fear of death. Fear compounds the problem, and your enemy knows it.

I want to explain how cortisol, a stress hormone, can affect the immune system. I want you to understand that Satan knows exactly how to destroy our immune system because of sin. Fear is sin. Bitterness is sin. When there is an excessive secretion of cortisol due to fear, interleukin-2—which is the product in the cell that identifies other cells as friend or foe, as I explained earlier—is devalued. In other words, fear increases cortisol which destroys interleukin-2.

Cortisol is always released long-term in the resistance stage of the General Adaptation Syndrome of fear, anxiety and stress. If we are constantly geared up to fight an enemy that we have never defeated, and we worry, then cortisol will be released long-term. It is the product of continuous stress and anxiety, looking over our shoulder, fear of death, fear of dying, fear of disease, fear of mother-in-laws, and pastorphobia. It is a lethal poison and Satan knows it.

Satan wants our blood. Satan wants the marrow of our bone because the Bible says the life of the body is in the blood.

> **For the life of the flesh *is* in the blood:**
>
> Leviticus 17:11

The life of the body is in the blood and Satan knows the Bible better than any pastor. He knows if he can get us into the sin of fear and anxiety, then he can get the malfunctioning of 1 John 4:18: there is no fear in love, and perfect love casts out fear.

> **There is no fear in love; but perfect love casteth out fear: because fear hath torment. He that feareth is not made perfect in love.** 1 John 4:18

Fear has torment. He that fears is not made perfect in love. Satan knows he can get us to look over our shoulder! We have abundant fears. We are constantly up in the air, looking over our shoulder, judging ourselves, questioning ourselves, comparing ourselves to others, not loving God, not loving ourselves, not loving our neighbor. We live in a cesspool of spiritual stench, a pollution of life when we are supposed to be the royal priesthood! But we are following another gospel.

The Word says you are not to fear what man or Satan can do. Put your trust in the Lord!

> **So that we may boldly say, The Lord *is* my helper, and I will not fear what man shall do unto me.**
> Hebrews 13:6

Satan knows he can get us to produce excessive cortisol. He knows if he can get us stewing in our juices about something or get us to begin to carry a record of wrongs about ourselves, God or others, then we are his.

Bitterness is not always about others. We can get into shame and guilt against ourselves. Everyone talks about forgiving others. Do you have unforgiveness and resentment against yourself? Are you holding yourself guilty from the past? How about unforgiveness and Bitterness toward God? It is deeper than you think. What about being afraid of God? Can you imagine being afraid of God?

Excessive cortisol produces death in T cells, white corpuscles, macrophages and killer cells. This is the immune system! We have a problem. We need it to destroy Cancer cells.

If we have fallen out of agreement with fear and have made our peace with God, ourselves and our brother—really, sincerely made our peace—we will have a healthy immune system. If we do not have fear of death, dying and disease and all the garbage that we are fighting in our soul and spirit, then cortisol will no longer be secreted. The T cells will begin to re-multiply and come back to proper strength. When that happens, interleukin-2 will be activated.

God has created us with a strong immune system so that every Cancer cell in our body, including any tumor of any size, will be eaten alive by T cells. But there is a condition. We must be well in our spirituality.

Remember the man from *Discover* Magazine? Where did all his Cancer go? His immune system got healed.

God has not given you the spirit of Fear, but power, love and a sound mind.

> **For God hath not given us the spirit of fear; but of power, and of love, and of a sound mind.**
>
> 2 Timothy 1:7

If our cortisol is not being oversecreted, then our T cells will eat the Cancer cells. Our T cells know what to eat because of the antigen flag. Everything that comes into our body, whether a virus or the foods we eat, has an antigen flag. The ability of our T cells to recognize the antigen flag on an invader such as a virus, bacteria, a rogue Cancer cell or even masses of Cancer cells—which are genetic mutations of creation in their own source—requires interleukin-2 as the activating chemical.

Satan knows he can make us sick if he can get us stewing in our stuff and out of sync with God's commandments of what creation should look like in relationship. He can leave us vulnerable for everything that is coming. We give him permission to do it in our disobedience.

I think it would be good to include spirituality in our nutrition. I think it would be good to eat spiritual manna as a way of life. Man shall not live by bread alone, but by every word that proceeds out of the mouth of God.

> **But he answered and said, It is written, Man shall not live by bread alone, but by every word that proceedeth out of the mouth of God.** Matthew 4:4

This scripture does not say we do not live by bread; it says man shall not live by bread *alone*. So mix the two mannas. It is not just a "hallelujah" diet; it is a heavenly diet!

ANTI-ONCOGENES

Now let's talk about anti-oncogenes and the immune system. The anti-oncogenes are immune enzymes of the immune system. They come in pairs in every cell. When we have both anti-oncogenes present in a cell, that cell will never develop Cancer. It is safe. The only way it can be compromised is through external or internal toxicity or viral invasion.

Viruses

Viruses often play a very important part in the development of Cancer because viruses are mutated genetic code material.

One of the medical community's most astounding definitions of viruses I have ever come across is this: *viruses are an alien genetic life force.* Viruses are genetic material, but behind the virus is an intelligence that defies imagination! Genetic code material does not think, but behind viruses is an invisible being that thinks.

We also completed a study on HIV. We discovered that mankind can come up with a medication or something to try to defeat this HIV virus, but the virus will see us coming before the medicine even goes into our bodies—like it has eyes! It takes its genetic form, which is its present strain of HIV, dips into the host genetic pool of tissues and extracts particular building blocks of RNA and DNA, and then remanufactures a different code. It stamps out different strains and is off laughing at us while we are trying to defeat something that is already dead. Behind the HIV virus is an intelligence that defies imagination.

In a person with genital herpes, for example, the virus can lie dormant for months and months and months until that person has a stress event. Then the virus is activated. What connection does stress have with a virus? Virus is an intelligence!

GENETIC CODE DEFECT

We were in British Columbia one year, and a lady came to me with a disease I had never heard of before. It was Charcot-Marie-Tooth Disease, a genetically inherited disease that produces a neuropathy of the nerve endings of the spine. When I began to sit down and look at my medical material, which I carry with me to seminars to research diseases I have never heard of, I came across an astounding observation.

Charcot-Marie-Tooth neuropathy of the nerve endings of the spine produces a type of dystrophy and a curling of the toes. It causes an inability to walk right, and it is very painful. While it is inherited at birth, the disease can develop in any decade of a person's life: the teens, 20's, 30's, 40's, 50's, 60's, 70's, and into the 80's. It is triggered by a stressful life event.

Do you understand what I am saying? *Behind even the release of genetic code defect is an invisible intelligence.* What connection does stress have to do with genetics? None.

When I went to sit down with this girl after I read the information in my medical journals, I looked at her and she said, "Did you find out anything about my disease?"

I said, "Yes, when did you get this disease?"

She told me it was about ten years earlier, at age 28.

I said, "So who jilted you, who abandoned you, who injured you emotionally and spiritually and broke your heart?"

She began to say, "How would you know this?"

I said, "Pretty easy." The *Merck Manual* says a life event can set in motion a genetic code movement to produce the disease in any decade of your life. It was not hard to figure it out. I just did not know the particulars. "How close am I?"

She said, "You know too much. You're right on the money." She started to weep, and I began to minister to her around this issue. Cancer is not much different.

We have found that a genetic code defect can be set into motion. I believe that many times there is a viral component to Cancer. There are people who say that Cancer is a virus. There is a mixed bag of thought about this, but I am fully convinced at this point in time, as a minister, that viruses are spirits of infirmity in the tissue. We at **Be in Health**™ have been approaching them as an intelligence and we have been getting some results.

So how do we deal with it? Well, first of all we cast out the spirit of Infirmity and take authority over tissue. Those are areas we can minister to, as well as genetic impurity. Every person at birth, where God is concerned, has both anti-oncogenes present in the cell tissue unless something internal or external destroyed these enzymes. Then the cell would become compromised, and mutation or mitosis can begin at any time.

We have what is called predisposed, or vulnerable, people. If there is inherited Cancer in a particular part of our body, it is in our family tree. We may have been born with a genetic predisposition and chromosome abnormality in the tissue structure where we have only one anti-oncogene. We may be born with one anti-oncogene. This cell is now predisposed, vulnerable and very susceptible to internal or external chemical invasion at the level which I have been teaching.

Mammograms and Breast Cancer

In our research several years ago, while downloading information from the AMA, we came across a startling statistic. Ten percent of all Breast Cancer in America is caused by mammograms. Why is 10 percent of all Cancer in America caused by mammograms? Because 10 percent of all females have inherited Breast Cancer, and when they get a mammogram, *the radiation destroys the anti-oncogene!* When the anti-oncogene is destroyed, the cell is compromised and Breast Cancer can begin.

Have you heard the discussion about mammograms causing Breast Cancer? We may read about it a little bit in the paper, but when we do research here, downloading every day, it is like a yo-yo: we should do mammograms; we should not. We should; we should not.

A few years ago, published medical reports stopped recommending mammograms, but they did not tell us why. They knew radiation was causing Breast Cancer. It has been for years.

It also depends on the technician giving the mammogram. We have had people come here and then go to the medical center to get a mammogram. I have asked the technician how many units of radiation (rad) they were going to use. They refused to tell us.

The maximum amount of radiation breast tissue should ever be exposed to in a lifetime is 100 rads. In a normal mammogram, depending on the technician, we can get from 0.50 to 48. Any woman that has a history of inherited Breast Cancer is incredibly susceptible to Cancer when they take a mammogram.

The first week after our daughter Abigail Ruth was born, we went to the gynecologist for my wife's checkup. I never let my wife go to a doctor without my being present. The nurse came in and said to her, "You know, especially at your age, you need to schedule a mammogram over at the med center immediately."

Well first of all, a mammogram should not be done on a breast-feeding mother. But she was adamant; I mean this nurse was Miss General! I sat there and listened—and felt the pressure. The average person off the street would think she knew what she was talking about.

I listened to this and felt the pressure coming and I finally had enough. I looked at the nurse and said, "Are you willing to take responsibility for my wife financially?"

She said, "What are you talking about?"

I said, "Have you tested my wife genetically to see if she is predisposed to Breast Cancer? Have you had an oncologist and/or geneticist test her?"

"Why is that necessary?" she asked.

I said, "AMA statistics. Ten percent of all Breast Cancer in America is caused by a mammogram, and this basically afflicts people who are predisposed genetically. Are you willing to take the responsibility? Forget the fact that she is a breast-feeding mother. Are you willing to take responsibility for the damages and the lawsuit that is coming if she gets Cancer?" That nurse disappeared and we never saw her again.

The Gift of Miracles

In our ministry to people with Cancer, we pray very specifically. We want restoration of what Father God saw in Christ Jesus in creation from the foundation of the world that has been damaged by sin. So we speak a creative miracle. In the gifts of the Holy Spirit we have the gift of healing and the gift of miracles.

> **9To another faith by the same Spirit; to another the gifts of healing by the same Spirit;**
> **10To another the working of miracles.**
> 1 Corinthians 12:9-10

Many people misunderstand these giftings. Why do we have the gift of miracles? First of all, God is the Creator, and parts of our body do not heal. If there is damage to our brain tissue, nerve tissue or to the organs of the body, then I am wasting my time praying for healing.

If I try to operate in the gift of healing, I am wasting my time because those organs do not heal. That is why they have organ transplants. So what do we do? We cannot minister healing because we are wasting our time. The Bible says *you have not because you pray amiss.*

> **Ye ask, and receive not, because ye ask amiss, that ye may consume *it* upon your lusts.** James 4:3

What is the gift of miracles? That's easy. Look at creation. Part of our body heals normally when that which is causing the problem is removed. The other part of the body does not heal at all because it is not possible. So in order to heal those parts of the body where it is not possible to heal, we have to operate in the gift of miracles.

So how does the gift of miracles work? First of all, it cannot heal, so we speak it into existence as if it were. We do it in His name.

> **(As it is written, I have made thee a father of many nations,) before him whom he believed, *even* God, who quickeneth the dead, and calleth those things which be not as though they were.** Romans 4:17

We had a case a year ago, right here in Georgia in an open church service, where God used me to grow out a young lady's arm 5 inches. She injured it in a fall from a tree 5 years before it had not grown in those 5 years because the growth plates were so damaged.

We watched for two minutes and before our eyes God formed every bit of that arm, including fatty tissue. That one arm was just like the other one. We were speaking things into existence, *calling those things that are not, as though they were,* in His name.

There is a testimony about an Organic Brain Syndrome when a lady had so many electro-shock therapy treatments in her journey that her IQ dropped almost 30 points. We all need every brain cell we have; God put them there for a reason! Operating in the gift of miracles, in the name of Jesus, I spoke into her every brain cell that had been destroyed by electro-shock therapy and God did it; her IQ jumped 30 points. Now she is a very smart woman again.

Could we speak, then, new ovaries into existence? Could we speak a new pancreas into existence because the old has been damaged by Diabetes? Could we speak into the genetics of disease, into genetic impurity in the name of Jesus? Could we command the anti-oncogenes that are missing, that cause a cell to be compromised from Cancer, to be formed and take authority over Cancer?

Could we deal with the spiritual roots and the blocks to healing? Could we speak that cell to be as it was from the foundation of the world in Christ Jesus? Yes we can, as believers. The reason it is not happening is because *we are not doing it.*

One of the biggest fallacies of Christianity is we are asking God to do it all. The Bible says those that believe shall do it in His Name. Yet, you hear people say, "Well, Jesus do this, and Jesus do that. Father do this…"

No, *you* do it, in His Name! Jesus says, "In that day you shall ask Me nothing."

> **And in that day ye shall ask me nothing. Verily, verily, I say unto you, Whatsoever ye shall ask the Father in my name, he will give *it* you.** John 16:23

Why are we praying to Jesus? "You shall ask Me nothing but you shall ask the Father in My name and He shall give to you whatsoever you ask."

We have a long way to go to reclaim the territory we have lost from Matthew, Mark, Luke, John and Acts.

You speak to genetic impurity! Command it to be reversed. If Satan can produce disease, God can heal it and change it. That is why I am teaching you about spiritual roots of disease and blocks to healing.

The number one block to healing is unforgiveness. We *have to forgive* our brother. We have no other choice. We might as well just cry, "Uncle." We can love the person, but still hate the sin. We have a right to hate the sin in someone that has hurt us, but we must forgive and love him. Can we see our problem? We have made the person evil too. That is not scriptural.

Have you read Romans chapter 7? Paul said it was not him doing it, but sin that lives within him was doing it.

> **Now then it is no more I that do it, but sin that dwelleth in me.** Romans 7:17

An Inherited Factor

Here is one more thing I want to get across from new research. We have been ministering to many children with tumors which are present as these children come out of the womb. In this situation, there has to be an inherited factor.

We are really getting encouraged. We have documented evidence of brain tumors disappearing through our ministry here, in the practical applications of what we know about the roots of disease! We have had some tremendous success with tumors and we want more, especially with brain tumors.

This is from Johns Hopkins Intellihealth.com, dated February 20, 2002:

> A virus that infects about 65% of all children by the age of 14 may play a role in the development of the most common type of malignant brain tumor found in the young. This is called the JC virus. It is in a viral group called the Neurotrophicpolyoma Viruses...

> ...It typically infects the upper respiratory system the same way as the common cold, with airborne particles. "It is very common," he said. "Sixty-five to 70 percent of human populations worldwide get infected with this virus by age 14. So we all basically have this virus in our bodies. The virus causes no disease [no cancer, no tumors even in children] unless a patient's immune system is weakened or destroyed."

Susceptibility to viruses can produce Cancer. What causes the immune system to be destroyed? Children can be born with compromised immune systems. In recent research we have found something called the cortisol wash, which flushes the baby's brain stem with a stress hormone at the birth canal. It damages the baby's immune system immediately upon birth.

Just recently we have been dealing with Cerebral Palsy. In the book, *A More Excellent Way*™, you can read about my investigation, which indicated Cerebral Palsy was caused by injury in the birth canal or by a mother who had German Measles. This is what the medical community had said for years.

New research does not indicate that at all. In fact, a pediatrician from Alaska gave me the insight from medical research that says Cerebral Palsy is now considered to be an autoimmune disease that afflicts the child *in utero* during the fourth month. In this case the mother's immune system, uniting with the child's, begins to attack the neurological processes, to eat it, destroy it and cause damage.

As we have begun to do case studies on this subject, we are finding these mothers had a conflict in their marriages, in their lives, and in their homes during the fourth month of pregnancy. Guilt, shame, self-hatred, and self-rejection were found to be strong in every female we looked at. These spiritual mechanisms in Cerebral Palsy make it an autoimmune disease where the body destroys itself.

Cancer Profile

Now as I begin to conclude these new insights on Cancer, I want to read some notes I have on the Cancer Profile. I am not going to discuss the various types of Cancers I deal with because they are in *A More Excellent Way*™. Those I deal with primarily include Breast Cancer—which also in a similar vein includes fibroid tumors, breast cysts and uterine cysts. We also deal with Colon Cancer, Uterine Cancer, Leukemia and Hodgkin's disease, to name a few. In all of these Cancers, we have found very specific spiritual roots. These are both inherited traits and personality traits.

The person who fits the Cancer Profile denies certain strong needs and represses a lot of feelings. What is often found in people who develop Cancer is they shut down. They do not want to be hurt anymore, so they end up in a denial state, suppressing everything. We would call that internalizing the rage, anger and bitterness. There is hopelessness and despair that goes with it that helps them shut down because there does not seem to be any solution.

The Cancer profile also involves people who are not very good at handling anger, who respond to stress with awful feelings of hopelessness, helplessness and despair. That person is therefore very vulnerable to developing Cancer.

Cancer is not just a disease coming out of nowhere, even though there are specific environmental issues such as external toxins, which certainly would play a part. We are talking about the spiritual spectrum of disease right now.

Cancer is not a disease developing out of a single, specific root cause. Apart from the actions of chemical invasion from the outside, a large percentage of Cancers are the result of converging factors involving spiritual and personality traits, along with stressful life events that are never changed or resolved.

In a Cancer-prone individual, a certain combination of these traits makes them especially vulnerable, both in their personal lives and in their family trees. This is an inherited factor.

The following characteristics are observable in the spirituality and the psychology of Cancer-prone individuals:

1. A marked inability to forgive.

2. A tendency towards self-pity and self-introspection.

3. A poor ability to develop and maintain meaningful, long-term relationships without fear.

4. A great tendency to hold resentment.

5. Poor self image.

These areas make it difficult for a person to deal with their own thoughts at a conscious level, or to acknowledge and deal with negative feelings. The other possible doorpoints that have been observed in case histories are:

1. The loss of a serious love object up to 24 months prior to onset, or continued grief and unresolved issues relative to the love object.

2. The loss of a significant life role or purpose.

3. Getting fired or being rejected in vocational or avocational pursuits. Loss of hope. Hope deferred.

The Bible says hope deferred makes the heart sick. Look at the scripture:

> **Hope deferred maketh the heart sick: but *when* the desire cometh, *it is* a tree of life.** Proverbs 13:12

That tree within is the life of God. Even when the prophet Jeremiah, mully-grubbing in his self-pity and bemoaning the day his mother ever conceived him and that he was ever born, turns around right in the middle and says, "Yes, but there is a fire that burns within me that cannot be quenched." So much for his self-pity and so much for introspection!

The Cancer Profile person responds to loss, whatever that looks like, with profound feelings of helplessness and hopelessness. Then there are other defense mechanisms that begin to come to help them protect themselves from this inner battle. Their feelings are not acknowledged inwardly. They are in denial with themselves about their own feelings.

Sometimes they put on a fabricated personality. They will put on a smile, but it is not a real smile. They will put on all kinds of defense mechanisms to hide the real pain within. These feelings are not expressed to others.

The Bible says to confess our faults one to another so that *we may be healed.*

> **Confess *your* faults one to another, and pray one for another, that ye may be healed. The effectual fervent prayer of a righteous man availeth much.** James 5:16

The Cancer Profile person does not trust others who might reject them and therefore does not do well in confession. So they do not confess. They internalize their problems and their weaknesses. Another aspect is the person may put on a happy face and deny any sense of loss, anger, distress, disappointment or despair.

Listen to this medical statement: Malignancy at the cellular level (which is what Cancer is) is despair that has been experienced biologically. It may be seen, then, that none of us just *gets* Cancer. We reach a point at which our deepest need and wish is to withdraw from life, and we therefore choose to develop Cancer. This is truth, although we would openly and aggressively deny that as truth.

I suggest that we become aggressive in dealing with the existence of Cancer and what causes it. Begin to fight!

> **I call heaven and earth to record this day against you, *that* I have set before you life and death, blessing and cursing: therefore choose life, that both thou and thy seed may live:** Deuteronomy 30:19

> **For as he thinketh in his heart, so *is* he: Eat and drink, saith he to thee; but his heart *is* not with thee.** Proverbs 23:7

It is possible many Cancers are a state of despair made manifest and real. How then do our spirituality and thoughts get translated into malignant cells? The link between mind and body is the body's natural defense system, which is our immune reaction to anything foreign or abnormal in the blood. It is a failure in the immune defense system that may allow the Cancer to develop and grow.

It is estimated aberrant cells may develop at least 200 times in a person's lifetime. If the immune system is healthy, then immune mechanisms reject these cells in their early state of tumor formation by surrounding and destroying them. The immune defense system constantly watches over our interior milieu, defending us from within, unless the integrity of the immune mechanisms has been compromised. This can happen under the pressure of chronic spiritual and soul stress.

The immune system can be adversely affected by our thoughts through two pathways, first, through the central nervous system via the limbic system, which includes the hypothalamus. (There is a direct suppressive link from thought to the health of the immune system.) The other pathways are the endocrines and hormones: the endocrine system is also managed by the limbic system and by the hypothalamus. Hormonal imbalances created by improper thoughts and emotions further suppress the immune system and its responses.

In fact, if bad thinking can cause disease, then the reverse of this equation could also be true:

Good thinking can prevent disease,
Cancer included!